HAL•LEONARD®

SAXOPHONE PLAY-ALONG

VOL. 10

JOHN COLTRANE

AUDIO ACCESS INCLUDED

PLAYBACK+
Speed • Pitch • Balance • Loop

T0065924

CONTENTS

Cover photo by Leni Sinclair/Getty Images

To access audio visit:
www.halleonard.com/mylibrary

Enter Code
5441-0814-0691-2234

Musicians:
Trumpet – Jamie Breiwick
Saxophone – Jason Weber
Drums – Devin Drobka
Bass – John Christensen
Piano – Mark Davis

Blue Train
(Blue Trane)
By John Coltrane

F7#9

C — F7#9   B♭7#11

F7#9   B♭7#11

F7#9

C7#9   F7#9

D   F7#9   B♭7#11   F7#9

B♭7#11

F7#9   C7#9

F7#9

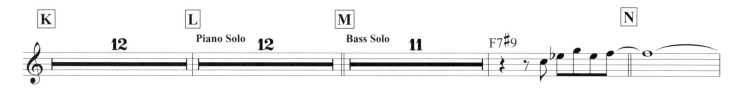

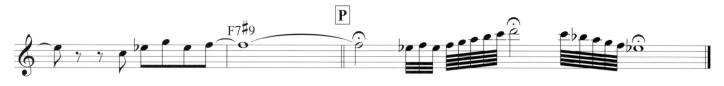

Cousin Mary

By John Coltrane

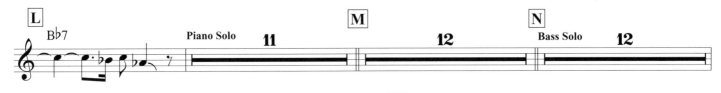

Body and Soul

Words by Edward Heyman, Robert Sour and Frank Eyton
Music by John Green

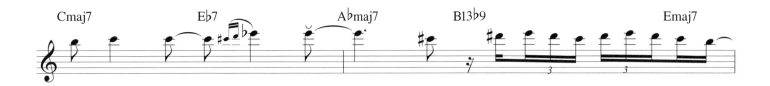

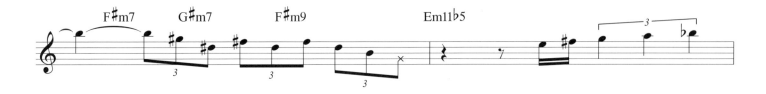

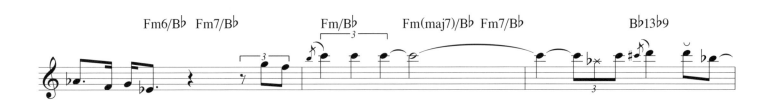

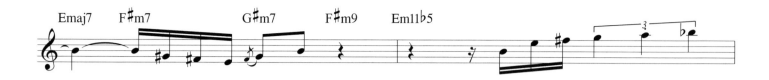

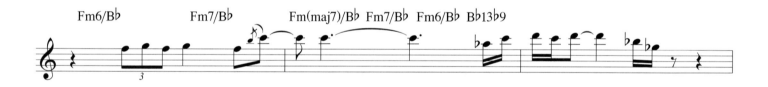

C7#5(b9)

Slowly (Rubato)

Fm9

Dm7   G7#5(b9)

Fm9   Bb13b9   **Moderately Slow**

Ebmaj7   Gmaj7   Bmaj7

Fm7   Bb13b9   Ebmaj7 Abmaj7   Gm7   Fm7

Very Slow (Rubato)
Ebmaj7

Central Park West

By John Coltrane

Giant Steps

By John Coltrane

Fingered as D, overtone sounds as A

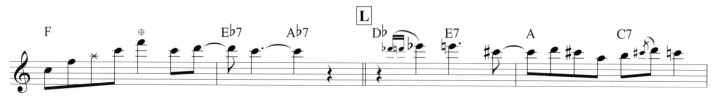

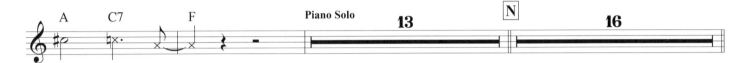

My Favorite Things

Lyrics by Oscar Hammerstein II
Music by Richard Rodgers

C

D

* Side "D"

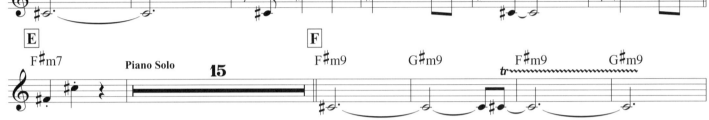

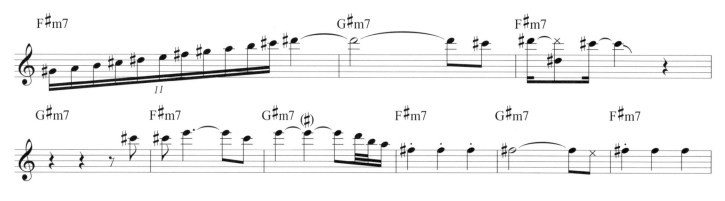

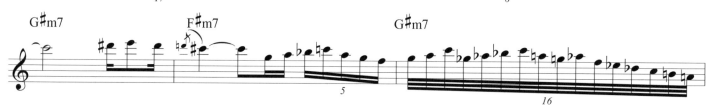

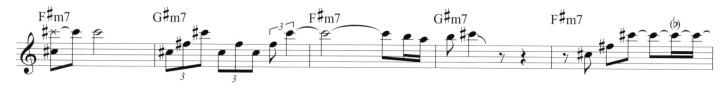

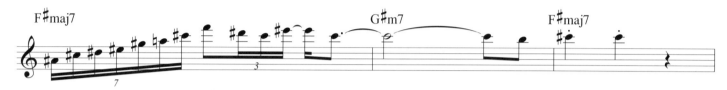

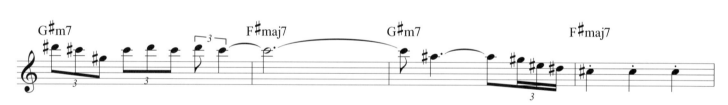

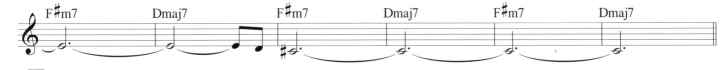

Like Sonny
(Simple Like)

By John Coltrane

Dbmaj7   Fm7   Bb7

I Em7   Gm7

Bbm7

C7b9   Fmaj7

J Em7

Gm7   ⊕   RUSH   Bbm7

C7b9   Fmaj7

Bm7

Gm7

K Ebm7   Ab7

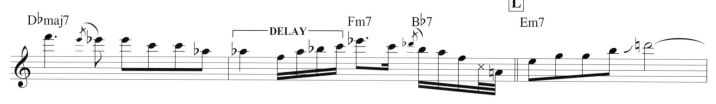

                                                L

Dbmaj7   DELAY   Fm7   Bb7   Em7

Naima
(Niema)

By John Coltrane

Fm7

Bmaj7/F   Amaj7/F   B♭maj7/F

Cm7/F

Fm7   Bm7/F   Amaj7/F

B♭maj7/F   D♭maj7/C

C13♭9   D♭maj7/F

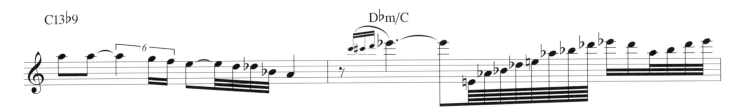

C13♭9   D♭m/C

D♭maj7/C   B♭maj7/C

C

A♭13/C   Cm7/F

DELAY

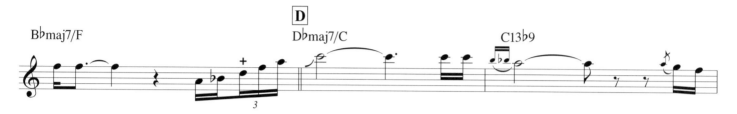

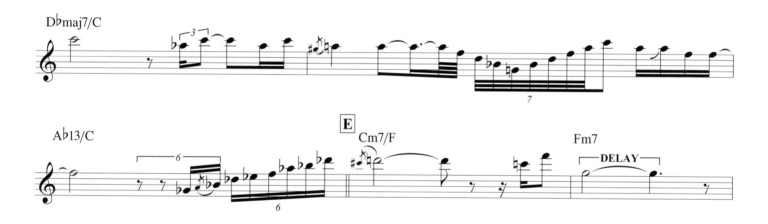

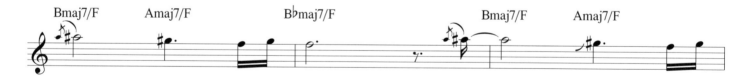

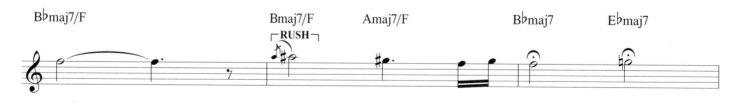

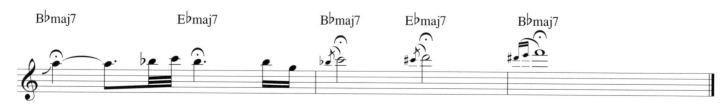

Blue Train
(Blue Trane)

By John Coltrane

Eb Saxophone

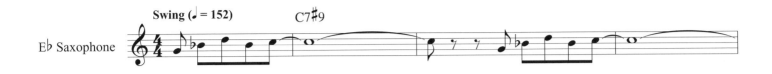

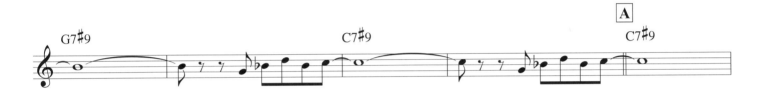

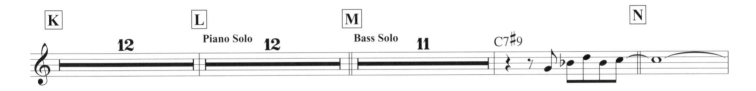

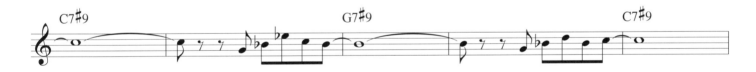

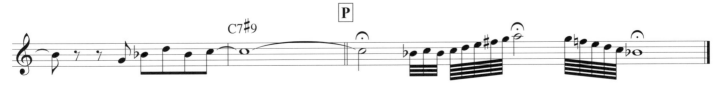

Body and Soul

Words by Edward Heyman, Robert Sour and Frank Eyton
Music by John Green

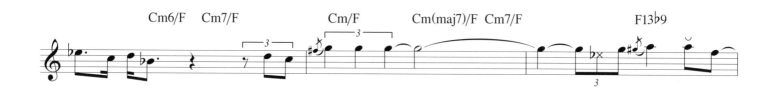

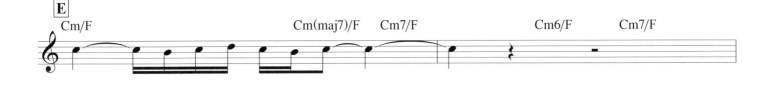

Piano Solo **29**

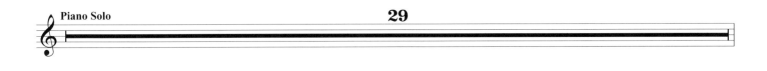

G

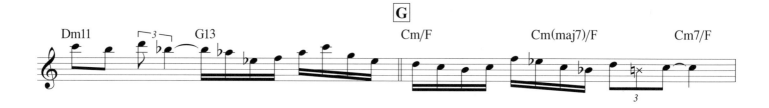

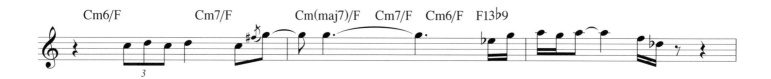

Slowly (Rubato)

Very Slow (Rubato)

Central Park West

By John Coltrane

Cousin Mary

By John Coltrane

Straight Ahead (♩ = 226)

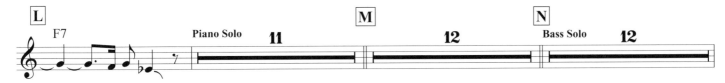

Giant Steps

By John Coltrane

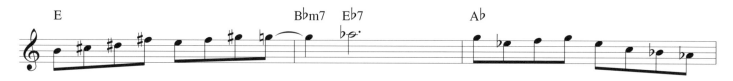

* Fingered as A, overtone sounds as E

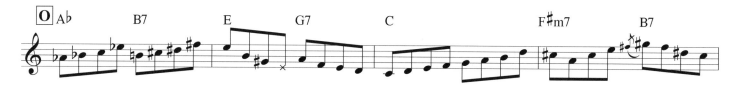

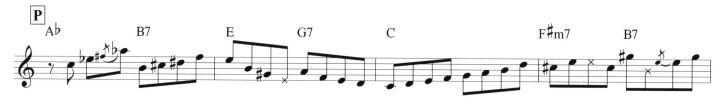

Q Head

R

Like Sonny
(Simple Like)
By John Coltrane

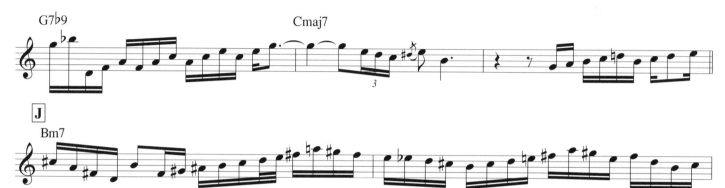

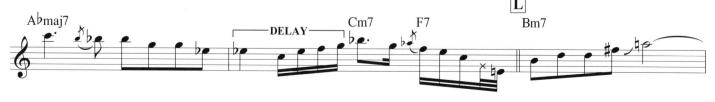

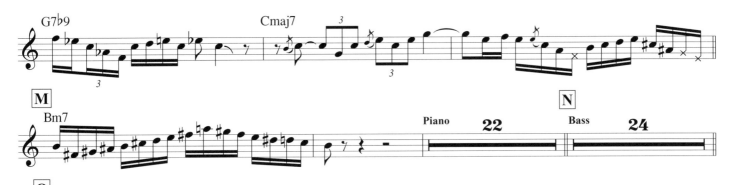

My Favorite Things

Lyrics by Oscar Hammerstein II
Music by Richard Rodgers

$\downarrow$ is slightly longer than $\downarrow$

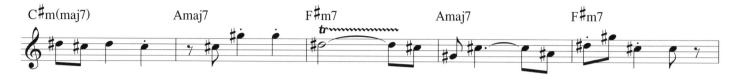

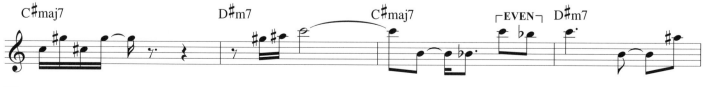

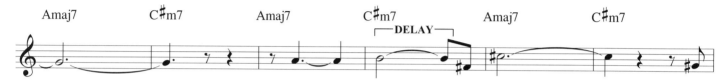

Naima
(Niema)

By John Coltrane

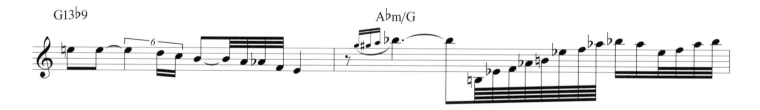

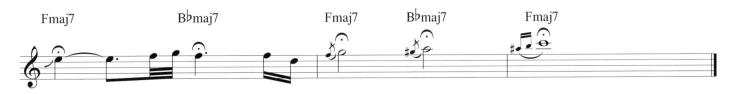

HAL•LEONARD SAXOPHONE PLAY-ALONG

The Saxophone Play-Along Series will help you play your favorite songs quickly and easily. Just follow the music, listen to the audio to hear how the saxophone should sound, and then play along using the separate backing tracks. Each song is printed twice in the book: once for alto and once for tenor saxes. The melody and lyrics are also included. The audio CD is playable on any CD player but it can also be used in your computer to adjust the recording to any tempo without changing pitch! Books with online audio also include **PLAYBACK+** options such as looping and tempo adjustments.

1. ROCK 'N' ROLL
Bony Moronie • Charlie Brown • Hand Clappin' • Honky Tonk (Parts 1 & 2) • I'm Walkin' • Lucille (You Won't Do Your Daddy's Will) • See You Later, Alligator • Shake, Rattle and Roll.
00113137 Book/CD Pack.. $16.99

2. R&B
Cleo's Mood • I Got a Woman • Pick up the Pieces • Respect • Shot Gun • Soul Finger • Soul Serenade • Unchain My Heart.
00113177 Book/CD Pack.. $16.99

3. CLASSIC ROCK
Baker Street • Deacon Blues • The Heart of Rock and Roll • Jazzman • Smooth Operator • Turn the Page • Who Can It Be Now? • Young Americans.
00113429 Book/Online Audio $16.99

4. SAX CLASSICS
Boulevard of Broken Dreams • Harlem Nocturne • Night Train • Peter Gunn • The Pink Panther • St. Thomas • Tequila • Yakety Sax.
00114393 Book/Online Audio. $16.99

5. CHARLIE PARKER
Billie's Bounce (Bill's Bounce) • Confirmation • Dewey Square • Donna Lee • Now's the Time • Ornithology • Scrapple from the Apple • Yardbird Suite.
00118286 Book/Online Audio....................................... $16.99

6. DAVE KOZ
All I See Is You • Can't Let You Go (The Sha La Song) • Emily • Honey-Dipped • Know You by Heart • Put the Top Down • Together Again • You Make Me Smile.
00118292 Book/Online Audio $16.99

7. GROVER WASHINGTON, JR.
East River Drive • Just the Two of Us • Let It Flow • Make Me a Memory (Sad Samba) • Mr. Magic • Take Five • Take Me There • Winelight.
00118293 Book/Online Audio $16.99

8. DAVID SANBORN
Anything You Want • Bang Bang • Chicago Song • Comin' Home Baby • The Dream • Hideaway • Slam • Straight to the Heart.
00125694 Book/Online Audio $16.99

9. CHRISTMAS
The Christmas Song (Chestnuts Roasting on an Open Fire) • Christmas Time Is Here • Count Your Blessings Instead of Sheep • Do You Hear What I Hear • Have Yourself a Merry Little Christmas • The Little Drummer Boy • White Christmas • Winter Wonderland.
00148170 Book/Online Audio $16.99

10. JOHN COLTRANE
Blue Train (Blue Trane) • Body and Soul • Central Park West • Cousin Mary • Giant Steps • Like Sonny (Simple Like) • My Favorite Things • Naima (Niema).
00193333 Book/Online Audio $16.99

11. JAZZ ICONS
Body and Soul • Con Alma • Oleo • Speak No Evil • Take Five • There Will Never Be Another You • Tune Up • Work Song.
00199296 Book/Online Audio $16.99

HAL•LEONARD®

Visit Hal Leonard online at **www.halleonard.com**

Prices, contents, and availability subject to change without notice. 1116